Blogs, Wikis, and Podcasts, Oh My!

Electronic Media in the Classroom

Authors

Jeffrey Piontek, M.S.Ed.

Blane Conklin, Ph.D.

SHELL EDUCATION

BLOGS, WIKIS, AND PODCASTS, OH MY!

Associate Editors
Roberta Chewning
Torrey Maloof

Editorial Director
Dona Herweck Rice

Editor-in-Chief
Sharon Coan, M.S.Ed.

Editorial Manager
Gisela Lee, M.A.

Creative Director
Lee Aucoin

Cover Design
Lee Aucoin

Production Manager
Don Tran

Interior Layout Design
Robin Erickson

Print Production
Robin Erickson

Publisher
Corinne Burton, M.A.Ed.

Shell Education

5301 Oceanus Drive
Huntington Beach, CA 92649-1030

http://www.shelleducation.com

ISBN 978-1-4258-0112-0

© 2009 *Shell Education*

Made in U.S.A.

"If we teach today's students as we taught yesterday's, we rob them of tomorrow."

—*John Dewey*

ACKNOWLEDGEMENTS

I would like to say thank you to all those who have allowed me to benefit from their wisdom, experience, and time. Many people have influenced me during my career as an educator and as a person. To my loving wife, Gabrielle, and my children, Noelle and Jonathan, who have supported me throughout this— as I was obsessed with actually getting it done. Without your patience, understanding, and support, this book would not have been possible. To my parents and immediate family who have lived through my development into the 40-something-year-old adolescent I am today, thanks for all the love and confidence you've shown in me.

I would especially like to thank three others. Dennis Pradier, my former superintendent and mentor, for your guidance, friendship, and support. This book never would have been possible without your assistance. To Alan November, thanks for being my friend, mentor, and colleague. You prove that alone we can make a difference, but together we can change the world. Thanks also to Stan Silverman from the New York Institute of Technology, who has been involved in technology since before I was born. You still have the passion and expertise to guide people like me to do our best for our teachers and our school children. There are too many other friends, colleagues, and mentors to mention. I thank all of you for your guidance and support.

To the teachers and students I have worked with over the years, thank you for allowing me to learn with you and from you. We can change the world one teacher and one student at a time. Never give up.

Jeffrey Piontek

My thanks goes to Dona Rice for her confidence in this project. I am happily indebted to my wife, Wendy, for her encouragement and support. She outshines me in everything she does, and inspires me to be better.

Blane Conklin

TABLE OF CONTENTS

#50112—*Blogs, Wikis, and Podcasts, Oh My!* © *Shell Education*

Foreword

#50112—*Blogs, Wikis, and Podcasts, Oh My!*

First and foremost, *Blogs, Wikis, and Podcasts, Oh My!* is a teacher-friendly book. As educators, we have all picked up technology how–to books and (1) felt bored because the book moved at a snail's pace and explained every minute detail, (2) felt angry because the book was written by an arrogant techie who talked down to the reader, (3) felt confused because the information was presented poorly, or (4) all of the above! We felt reading *Blogs, Wikis, and Podcasts, Oh My!* was time well spent. It contains well-written details to permit understanding and provides concrete suggestions, so a teacher can immediately carry out a lesson with his or her class.

Frankly, it is not surprising that Jeff's book is teacher friendly. Jeff Piontek was a classroom teacher for many years, and he works on a daily basis with teachers in their classrooms. Jeff is a teacher first and a techie second. His goal is not to wow us with technological jargon, but rather to provide us with practical, concrete information—examples, stories, etc.—that a teacher can actually use and understand. Jeff's tone and locutions are conversational; indeed, you can take the lad out of Brooklyn, but you can't take Brooklyn out of the lad!

Blogs, Wikis, and Podcasts, Oh My! is an important book for teachers. K–12 educators need to know about the emerging modes of communication. Technology has caused, and is causing, huge changes in the way we lead our daily lives. CDs, pay phones, and the *World Book Encyclopedia* are just about extinct. Online shopping and bill paying, Googling for information, and Skyping to friends internationally are daily facts of life. More to the point, however, Jeff's book is about what students are already doing every day with this new emerging online technology. According to a Pew Internet & American Life Project's recent survey of youth in the United States, students are spending 27 hours a week online at home, and an average of 15 minutes a week at school.

Why should students go online at school? As Jeff points out, online technologies such as blogs, wikis, and Skype, "give you a voice." They enable teachers and students not to just consume information, but to participate in the great worldwide conversation. Have a comment about the war in Iraq? Add a comment to a war news blog or participate in a wiki site on the war. That first time might feel scary—indeed, the whole world is watching! But one learns through discussion, and by using these online technologies, teachers and students gain the opportunity to participate in the ongoing, online grand conversation. What could be more motivating to a student to learn and get the facts straight than adding a comment to a news blog that enhances the entry? You simply can't do that with a textbook!

Access to computers and online resources in school remains a challenge. However, with the low-cost mobile computing devices quickly appearing on the market, the access challenge may well recede into history. But the current limitations don't stop resourceful educators. They can figure out how to accumulate online time for our students' use and do some of the activities suggested in Jeff's fine book.

Blogs, Wikis, and Podcasts, Oh My! is fun—fun to read, fun to think about, and fun to put into practice. By reading Jeff's book, educators can be more successful, more self-confident, and more effective in helping their students learn. And seeing students become successful is surely the greatest joy for an educator!

—Cathleen Norris and Elliot Soloway

Dr. Cathleen Norris is a Regents Professor in the Department of Learning Technologies, College of Education at the University of North Texas, and co-founder and Chief Education Architect of GoKnow! Inc, a company that develops K–12 resources for mobile computing devices.

Dr. Elliot Soloway is an Arthur F. Thurnau Professor at the University of Michigan and GoKnow! co-founder and CEO. They are both members of the LeapFrog SchoolHouse Educational Advisory Board.

Introduction

#50112—Blogs, Wikis, and Podcasts, Oh My! © Shell Education

In a high-speed, high-tech world, we must assure that our students are prepared for the challenges of the future and the global community we inhabit. This book will help teachers and administrators effectively use the Internet both in their own professional development and in the classroom with their students.

- Chapter 1 is an invitation to digital literacy. The twenty-first century learner needs skills to effectively find and evaluate information.

- Chapter 2 discusses the effective use of blogs in the classroom. This chapter will walk you through the creation of a blog and tips for making it a tool to enhance student learning.

- Chapter 3 introduces wikis. It will help you discover how to make wikis an effective classroom tool.

- Chapter 4 explores podcasting. It will discuss the tools to help you create audio and video files, and ways in which you can effectively use this technology in your classroom. This chapter and the next are based on the work of award-winning author and speaker Alan November.

- Chapter 5 is about other tools that will improve your connectivity in the digital age. It covers RSS feeds, Skype, and social bookmarking. These tools can influence the way we learn and utilize information.

- Chapter 6 is a brief conclusion.

- Appendix A contains a variety of valuable resources to help you and your students explore the world of technology in depth.

- Appendix B provides a complete list of cited references found within this book, as well as additional references used to support understanding of technology in the classroom.

#50112—*Blogs, Wikis, and Podcasts, Oh My!* © *Shell Education*

CHAPTER 1

An Invitation
to
Digital
Literacy

#50112—*Blogs, Wikis, and Podcasts, Oh My!*   © *Shell Education*

From the time they drag themselves out of bed until they finally crash to sleep at night, many of your students will navigate their day amid the buzz of a digital world. They'll connect with friends through one medium or another, texting, instant messaging, and emailing. They will reach out further with social networking sites such as Facebook, SecondLife, or MySpace. They will find and share games, movies, photos, music, and other entertainment.

As educators, we appreciate the need for students to unplug and "power down" when they enter the classroom. But perhaps we can take inspiration from the way they experience the world. As they unplug, we need to plug into teaching strategies that take advantage of the digital world and help prepare students to make the most of it.

An increasing number of students see school as disconnected from their fast-paced, highly interactive social environment where they have an active role in content development. But these tools and these types of interactions can actually help bring your class to life. Consider the possibilities of having your students come to class looking forward to plugging in and connecting in ways they never imagined possible in school. Such a bold move will surely make your classroom more engaging and relevant to their lives. The key is to find ways to diversify and utilize the kinds of media that students experience in their digitally-connected world outside school. We need to take what is essential in our curriculum and integrate it with what students find engaging. If we can keep an open mind and learn to become students again, we can add more rigor and relevance to the learning experience. Students are naturally more comfortable in the digital world, so if we allow them to take more ownership in their education by utilizing the tools they know best, we can actually learn from them.

This digital age demands a vision of education in which the learners lead their own learning. Such a vision is a necessity for our children to be competitive in the global digital age of the 21st century. For such a vision to succeed, it will require courageous educators willing to explore the strengths and weaknesses of these tools—tools that our students already use—to assist in the development of this new vision for education (NCTE 2008).

No matter what your current level of confidence in technology may be, you will profit from this resource. We have written this book for the teacher who has at least a basic knowledge of the Internet and uses email. The tools and ideas you acquire here will help you both in your own professional development and in your classroom with students. They will enhance communication and collaboration in your classroom and with your students' parents.

The guiding principal throughout this book is that nothing replaces jumping in, exploring, and experimenting with these technologies. For each of the tools we introduce, there are several different services available on the Web for you to investigate. The best services are easy to use and provide excellent instructions for the beginner. The Web is the ultimate "learn at your own pace" environment. If the first blog service you try seems to meet your needs, you can stop there. If you're happy with the basic setup, keep it that way. But if you're more experienced and confident, you can experiment with three or four services referenced in this book. You might actually build an elaborate wiki that will be a model for your entire school or district.

Before we jump into the deep end, there are some general ideas you should consider regarding Internet research and your students. For example, we were taught not to judge a book by its cover. The same holds true for websites and digital media. Sites that look important may not be important at all. Sometimes, it is difficult to get students to look beyond the colors, pictures, cool flash animations, and graphics to examine the actual content. However, this critical step can help eliminate spurious websites and invalid information.

Just like print material, it is sometimes difficult to know if you are reading fiction, nonfiction, editorials, or advertisements on the Internet. Therefore, asking questions and thinking critically about the information on the screen is imperative.

Here is a list of guiding questions to consider when judging Internet content:

- Is the information on the website useful for your topic?
- Are additional resources and links provided? Do the links work?
- Is the site current? When was it last updated?
- Do you think the information is accurate? Does the information contradict information you have found elsewhere?

When presenting these questions to your students, provide them with a list of websites to evaluate along with a copy of the guiding questions. You may want to add or modify these to ensure that the questions address the level of cognitive demand that you would expect along with the level of rigor. Some of our favorite sites are listed in Appendix A: Resources.

In the traditional print world, there is a multitude of books and magazines with varying quality and reliability. The same is true on the Internet. The skills you exercise when you evaluate a newspaper, textbook, or television news story are the same skills you use to evaluate a source on the Web.

Sources that you trust in the non-web world are usually available on the Web. You can find familiar faces such as *National Geographic*, *TIME Magazine*, *The Wall Street Journal*, or CNN, in an online format.

Beware especially when researching a controversial topic or figure. You will not likely find many intentional falsehoods when you look for gardening tips or facts on the solar system. However, if you are trying to find factual information about the life of Martin Luther King, Jr., or the presidency of George W. Bush, you need to know the source of your information. To check or verify facts or claims on the Internet, there are several reliable tools to use. Snopes.com (**http://snopes.com/**) specializes in urban myths and rumors. FactCheck.org (**http://www.factcheck.org/**) is specifically for political fact checking.

Wikipedia has quickly grown to become one-stop shopping for many people doing basic Internet research. Wikipedia may be a valuable tool in the *beginning* of research, but it is only a beginning. You should always examine other sources for information.

To verify the reputation of a source on a website, research the author and publisher of both the content and the website itself. If you ever want to know who owns the site or has published the material, try **http://www.easywhois.com**. Enter a domain name, and it returns information about the date this site was created along with specific contact names and addresses where the organization is based. This tool has limited value because people can easily hide behind valid web-hosting organizations. But this, too, can be a clue. If you have trouble determining the author of an article, a blog, or a website, your suspicions about the content may be legitimate.

Investigating links to websites is an important validating step because it can sometimes help students evaluate whether a site contains biased, false, or quality information. You can check the URLs of links by moving your cursor over a highlighted portion or graphic. The arrow will turn into a hand, and a URL appears in the status bar at the lower left of your browser.

When it comes to Internet security, the first line of protection will be the Information Technology office (or something similar) at your local school or organization. It is responsible for software and guidelines to protect your computer from viruses and inappropriate websites. Be sure to follow its guidelines and approach the office with any concerns you have about Internet safety and security at your school. Here are some sites that will provide you with more information:

- National Cyber Security Alliance: **http://staysafeonline.org/**

- Educause: **http://www.educause.edu/**

- International Society for Technology in Education: **http://www.iste.org/AM/Template.cfm**

The three chapters that follow will guide you through some Internet tools that will take you beyond the basics. Chapter 2 is about blogs, Chapter 3 covers wikis, and Chapter 4 introduces podcasts. Each technology we introduce will begin with a section entitled "Getting Started." Here we provide you with a basic orientation for using the tool and a list of free services to get you started. Keep in mind that new services and products emerge all of the time, so these lists will not be exhaustive. Though each service is a little different, we will not clutter the book with specific instructions for signing up for or using a particular service for several reasons. First, we do not want to endorse any particular product. Second, we do not want to limit you with our own preferences. Third, each service we list is reliable and provides simple instructions that any beginner can follow.

If you are already a user of any particular tool we discuss, you may skip the "Getting Started" section and move on to the second, "In the Classroom," which will provide you with tips and examples of how to use the tool with your students.

In Chapter 5, we round up a few more tools that you might find helpful: RSS feeds, Skype, and a social bookmarking tool. For these tools, we have chosen a representative service to explore, and we give you a quick introduction for setting up and using it in your daily routine.

Chapter 6 provides some concluding remarks and words of confidence. Finally, Appendix A lists a number of helpful resources for you and your students as you pursue these technologies in depth, and Appendix B provides a complete list of references cited in this book, as well as additional references used to support understanding of technology in the classroom.

#50112—*Blogs, Wikis, and Podcasts, Oh My!* © *Shell Education*

CHAPTER 2

Blogs

#50112—*Blogs, Wikis, and Podcasts, Oh My!* © *Shell Education*

The term *blog* is an abbreviation of "web log." Some blogs are like diaries but without the privacy. Many are used for reporting breaking news while others are an outlet for commentary and analysis. Whatever a blog may have in common with a log, journal, or diary, the important difference is that a blog is specifically intended for viewing by, and interacting with, someone other than the author.

The rationale for blogging is the same rationale for writing or communicating in general: to effectively participate as a knowledgeable member of society. This chapter discusses the creation, use, and effectiveness of blogs as instructional tools.

BLOGS: GETTING STARTED

Remember our first rule: The best way to learn is to jump in head first. So let's do it! First, pick one of the free blogging services below, or use another with which you are already familiar:

- Edublogs: **http://edublogs.org/**

- Blogger: **https://www.blogger.com/start**

- WordPress: **http://wordpress.com/**

- Live Journal: **http://www.livejournal.com/**

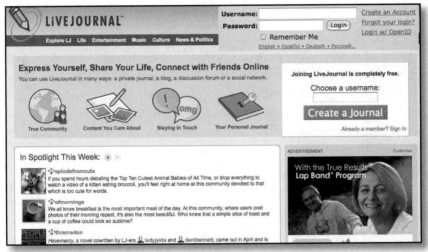

When you go to one of these sites, you will see a big button or link that says **Sign Up Here**, or something similar. Don't hesitate—sign up! You will need an email address to register for a blog. Feel free to start a blog on more than one service so you can compare the features and find the one that's best for you. Once you are registered, take time to look around, click links, push buttons, read tutorials, and get comfortable navigating around your blog.

It is easy to become overwhelmed by all the options available to you. However, if you pace yourself and start with the basics, you will become comfortable experimenting with more advanced functions later.

Each service is a little bit different, but the basic operation will be similar. You should post an entry to your blog as soon as possible, even if the title is "Testing" and the entry is just a sentence, "This is a test." This will allow you to see your blog in action. It is an exhilarating feeling to make changes to your blog and see immediate results.

Writing a blog entry is as easy as writing in any text editor. You can change the font, add colors, and format the text however you want. You can upload images, photos, videos, and artwork, and you can create links to other blogs or websites.

Another basic function of your blog is the comment area. Here, visitors can respond to your blog entry using a simple text box. Since the blog is viewable by the general public, you may want to change the settings to moderate any comments that are made. You can have an email notification sent to you whenever a comment is posted. Then you can decide whether you want to publish the comment.

Another option that may be available is to make your blog viewable only to those who have a special password, or those whom you specifically authorize to view it. However, this may require people to register with your service and log on each time they want to view your blog. This extra layer of privacy has its advantages, but the disadvantage is that it may discourage anyone from viewing your blog—even those you really want to visit. A better solution might be to keep your blog open to the public, monitor the comments, and make sure that you only post information about individual students that you want public.

Once you've gotten a good feel for posting entries and managing comments, you will want to play around with the layout, selecting colors and designs suited to your class. Find a "Settings" section and explore all the options available to you. In the sidebar of your blog, you can create a list of recommended links for your students.

BLOGS: IN THE CLASSROOM

As you will discover, the great thing about a blog is that it will help you easily do so many tasks that you already perform. It extends your reach, reinforces your efforts, and most importantly, it will make your students think that you are on the cutting edge of cool.

Three things to think about when you begin a blog are the author, the audience, and your purpose. First, there are several authors to consider. You as a teacher will become an expert blogger, but this is a skill that everyone in your classroom should learn. Once you have oriented yourself to the mechanics of the blog, get your students involved. Chances are they will adapt more quickly and easily than you did.

Second, you need to think about two primary audiences. Your students' parents constitute one potential audience, particularly for elementary grades. The other is your classroom, which includes both you and the students. Combining the two kinds of authors and two kinds of audiences, we have four possible lines of communication:

- Teacher to Parents
- Teacher to Classroom
- Students to Parents
- Students to Classroom

The third factor to consider with your blog is its purpose. Three of the most common functions of a classroom blog are to communicate information, promote discussion, and display work. When we throw these into the mix, it is apparent that each of the four combinations above could be used for at least two of these purposes:

- Teacher to Parents (information, present work)
- Teacher to Classroom (information, discussion)
- Students to Parents (information, present work)
- Students to Classroom (information, discussion, present work)

It is worth spending some time thinking about the best way for you to handle these possibilities for blogging in your classroom. Here are three models to consider.

ONE BIG HAPPY BLOG

You might consider creating a single multipurpose blog for your classroom. You can grant permission to your students to post entries, and it can be a central repository for news, discussion, and presentation of writings, artwork, and other student work. This might be the preferred model for primary grades, especially the youngest ones.

This model has two major advantages: one-stop navigation for parents and students, and the ability to update information often, keeping it fresh and interesting. However, whether you are a student or parent accessing this blog for particular information, it might appear chaotic. Parents looking for a news item will have to dig to uncover it, and if the blog is updated very often, students might feel a little overwhelmed.

MY BLOG, YOUR BLOG

Another model is to create different blogs for different authors. This might be as few as two—one for you and one for the students—or you might create a blog for each student. Remember that multiple blogs can be easily linked together. Each blog in your group can have a list of links to all the other blogs in the sidebar.

This model will naturally make more sense when your students can take a more active role—perhaps in middle and high school. As the teacher, you need to make sure that you have passwords for every account so you can monitor and edit any inappropriate content that may be posted on blogs representing your class. Beyond that, students should be responsible for managing and approving comments to their own blogs.

DIFFERENT BLOGS FOR DIFFERENT PURPOSES

You might choose to have one blog for news (regardless of whether the audience is parents or classroom), another for discussion and interaction between you and students, and yet another for students to present their own work. Again, for this last purpose you may opt for each student to create his or her own blog, or you might want to have a collective blog everyone can use. This model may be modified to combine news and discussion in a single blog.

It's completely up to you. Whatever model you choose to adopt, the possibilities for blogs in your classroom are limited only by your imagination. The following examples are just a few ideas to get you started.

1. Keep parents informed

Blogs can be used for communicating news and announcements to parents. Post an entry whenever you have something significant to share, but be sure to post something at least once a week. When parents visit the blog, they can ask questions or provide feedback by posting a comment. Your reply to comments within 24 hours is essential. It's important to be timely and up-to-date with your blog or it will become forgotten and irrelevant.

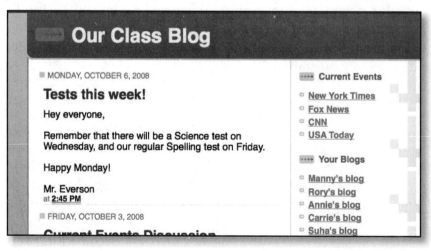

Our Class Blog

Saturday, December 27, 2008
Science Fair Reminder
Parents,

Remember to turn in the Science Fair Application for your child by Friday, January 9. Please let me know if you need another blank form, or if you have any questions.

thanks,
Ms. Collins

Current Events
- New York Times
- Fox News
- CNN
- USA Today

Your Blogs
- Manny's blog
- Rory's blog
- Annie's blog

2. News you can use

Your blog can be a medium for classroom news for your students. A post on Monday morning or over the weekend can be used to set up the coming week. This entry could include information such as birthdays for the coming week, who is responsible for watering the plants, reminders of upcoming tests and special events, or anything else you need to communicate to your students.

Our Class Blog

MONDAY, OCTOBER 6, 2008
Tests this week!

Hey everyone,

Remember that there will be a Science test on Wednesday, and our regular Spelling test on Friday.

Happy Monday!

Mr. Everson
at 2:45 PM

FRIDAY, OCTOBER 3, 2008

Current Events Discussion

Current Events
- New York Times
- Fox News
- CNN
- USA Today

Your Blogs
- Manny's blog
- Rory's blog
- Annie's blog
- Carrie's blog
- Suha's blog

3. Discussion starters or follow-ups

You can use a blog to pose questions and prompt discussion among your students. This might be a prelude to an upcoming lesson or a review of something you have already introduced. Topics could include current events, primary sources, editorials, or book reflections. Encourage students to post comments on their own time either at home or in the classroom. If you have students who do not have Internet access at home, give them priority time on classroom computers.

Here is an example of how to begin a discussion about a subject already covered in class courtesy of Heidi Jenkins, a fifth-grade teacher at Cactus Ranch Elementary in Round Rock, Texas.

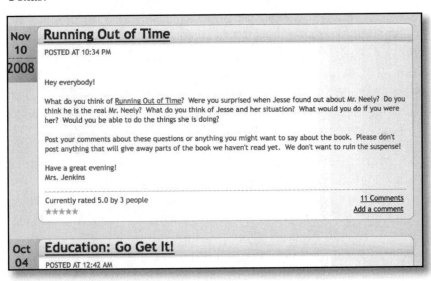

Here is an example of a new discussion starter.

> **Sep**
> **11**
> **2008**
>
> **Kids in Afghanistan**
> POSTED AT 10:37 PM
>
> Read the article below about a young girl living in Khewa, a district in Afghanistan. Think about her daily routine and how it is different from yours. Post your thoughts and comments.
>
> http://www2.scholastic.com/browse /article.jsp?id=5344

You might be surprised at both the quality and quantity of feedback you will receive through this medium. Students who are shy about contributing in front of the class may open up on the keyboard. Given the time to think about their response, most students will be able to compose a more thoughtful answer to the question than they would on the spur of the moment. Critical thinking skills will improve as students analyze and evaluate what you have posted.

Mary Beth Murgatroyd was a newcomer to these technological tools when she decided to take the plunge. She reports that her middle school students benefited greatly from a nightly book discussion on their classroom blog (Murgatroyd 2008). Her students began to show more initiative in their responses and gradually needed less guidance in the discussion. They learned the value of appreciating and respectfully interacting with different points of view. Their enthusiasm for the discussion increased the depth and quality of their responses, and Murgatroyd no longer needed to hound them to participate (Murgatroyd 2008).

4. Book reports

Students should learn to post their own blog entries, and book reports might be a good place to begin. You are probably already encouraging many non-traditional ways for students to report on books they read. Posting a blog entry could be added as one more option. The new format will encourage other students to take note of their classmates' reports. They will also be able to interact with classmates through the comment function of the blog, asking questions or giving encouragement to the reviewer.

5. Weekend update

Students can use their blogs to report news from a long weekend or vacation. While this can be a very informal kind of "show and tell" function of the blog, students should be encouraged to imagine writing for a large and diverse audience. This will help them improve their writing and guard against content that might be trivial or inappropriate.

6. Other writing projects

A blog is an excellent place to display poems and short stories created by students. Parents will appreciate being able to see their children's work online. Other students will be able to enjoy and compliment their classmates' work that they might not ordinarily see. Beyond these two primary audiences, a blog allows your students' creations to be appreciated by a wider public audience. Good literature and art are always welcome additions to the World Wide Web. Educators are noting that online tools are making students better writers (Phillips 2008). One reason is that students know they will have an audience other than just their teacher viewing their comments and entries. This extended audience also seems to encourage students who might otherwise lack confidence or motivation to begin writing (Collier 2008).

For privacy and security reasons, it is a good idea not to include last names or any other personal information about your students in your blogs. A first name is enough information to identify the author to primary audiences. If you have any students who prefer to keep their work viewable only to a selected audience, they may do so using whatever controls are available with the particular service you use. You, as the teacher, should always have full access to every blog.

As you can see, the potential for blogging is wide open. Now the ball is in your court. What will you do with blogs in your classroom and how will you manage and utilize this powerful tool?

CHAPTER 3

Wikis

#50112—*Blogs, Wikis, and Podcasts, Oh My!*   © *Shell Education*

The word *wiki* is of Hawaiian origin and means "quick." Wikis are online tools that allow users to collaborate and build a repository of knowledge. You are most likely familiar with the granddaddy of them all, Wikipedia (**http://www.wikipedia.org**). This wiki is an online encyclopedia that accepts all contributions. Anyone who wants to contribute a piece of information to a body of knowledge is free to do so.

You can create a wiki for your class. Whereas a blog is a tool suited for communication, discussion, and presentation, a wiki specializes in cooperative work toward something that will endure. The content of a blog is often time-sensitive and in-the-moment. The content of a wiki is usually more stable and lasting (though by no means permanent). Think of the difference between a news story and an encyclopedia entry. Unlike a print encyclopedia, however, a wiki can and should be updated frequently. A wiki is a living, growing body of knowledge that benefits from the efforts of many collaborators.

WIKIS: GETTING STARTED

As you might expect, wikis are better experienced than explained. Below are some of the best free wiki services on the Web. Choose one for now; you can try out the others later and see which one you like best.

- PBwiki: **http://www.pbwiki.com**

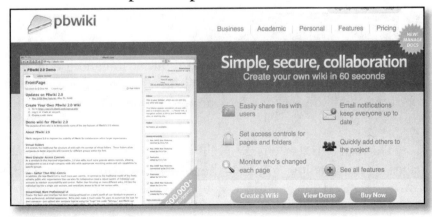

- Wikispaces: **http://www.wikispaces.com**

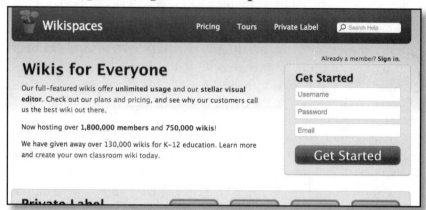

- Wetpaint: **http://www.wetpaint.com**

You will have no trouble figuring out how to sign up for your new wiki. Just look for the big bright button and follow the instructions. As with a blog, you will need an email address to register. View the tutorial, look around at the options, and take it for a spin!

The soul of the wiki is the ability to create countless different pages of information and link them any way you can imagine. You can upload images, documents, and other files you would like to incorporate. You will be able to see a complete history of who made changes and when. If you want to reverse a change, you can do that. These tools come with a discussion board, and you can have email updates sent to you whenever a change takes place or a comment is added.

As with blogs, you can adjust the settings of your wiki to limit who is able to view, update, and administer it. To maintain control over your wiki and distinguish among the authors, each of your students will need an email address.

Some free wiki services come with advertisements on the screen. You can upgrade to a paid service and avoid the ads. Upgrades also come with more storage space for files, and in some cases, more refined authorization features. Try the free versions of each service to see which one is best for you. You may find that you will be satisfied with the free version.

WIKIS: IN THE CLASSROOM

Just like blogs, the possibilities for wikis in your classroom are really wide open. In what kinds of projects would you love to see increased student participation? If you can come up with even one answer to that question, a wiki is your solution. Don't be afraid to experiment. If you don't like it, change it. That's the beauty of these online tools.

1. Research topics

The application of the wiki that most readily comes to mind (thanks to Wikipedia) is the encyclopedia-like accumulation of knowledge on a certain topic. Have each of your students contribute to a wiki about marine life, Asia, or U.S. presidents, but **do not** allow your students to consult Wikipedia. It will be too tempting to mimic the style or structure of that entry, and you want students to develop their own styles. Consult other online or printed sources. When you are finished with your project, compare and contrast it to Wikipedia.

- Wikipedia: **http://www.wikipedia.org**

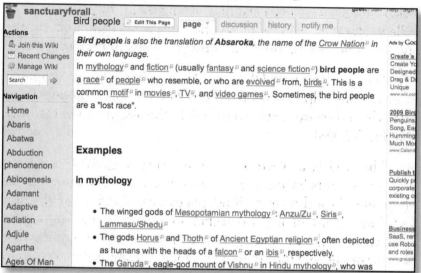

Take some time to think about the structure of your wiki (Morgan and Smith 2008). You want the front page to be a gateway and an introduction. It should have guidelines and policies for your student contributors. It should include a table of contents with links to each page so users and visitors can navigate directly to any part of the wiki from the front page. The structure of supporting pages might take some thought because it all depends on the project and your purpose. You might choose to give each student his or her own page. If you divide students into groups, each group might have one or more pages structured according to the outline chosen. Each situation will be unique, so just make sure that it is easy for users to see and access all that your wiki offers.

2. Writing projects

The wiki medium is well-suited to the writing process. The concepts of revision and multiple drafts are built into this technology. Having peers collaborate and comment on other students' writing guarantees that work will go through several versions.

Richard Smith arranged for his classroom to team up with Brian Morgan's college class in a writing/mentoring project. The college students were able to offer help and comments to the younger students via the wiki. Morgan and Smith report that:

"The students noted the ease of composition, the de-emphasis of error, the helpfulness of the collaboration, and the efficiency with which they were able to complete the assignments" (Morgan and Smith 2008).

The wiki is a place to exercise every stage of the writing process. Writers have often observed that one's first thoughts are often one's best thoughts. Students can use a wiki to brainstorm and dump a list of ideas or other loosely connected thoughts. They can use the same page to start formulating an outline or a plan for organizing these thoughts. Once a composition begins to emerge, editing and revising are convenient and welcoming.

Students can work individually or in groups. In her project with middle school students, Mary Beth Murgatroyd opted for groups of four (Murgatroyd 2008). They moved from blog discussions about a book to a wiki. Each group was assigned a page to create and develop. They had to come up with their own guidelines for collaboration, time management, and quality control. She was pleased with the degree of responsibility her students took and the impressive pages they created.

3. Library of reviews

Here is an idea that is a little more out of the box. Create a wiki of book reviews. Your front page could list all the books any of your students have read. Each title would link to a page of reviews by different students for that book. The list can be expanded to include books that no one in your class has yet read. This might be an incentive for students to read those books and write reviews.

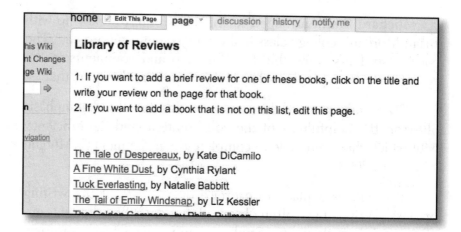

You might consider opening up this particular wiki to a wider community of contributors, perhaps other classes or grades in your school or another school. As long as you are diligent in screening participants and checking updates to the wiki, it can enrich your library of reviews. When your students discover reviews of the same books they have read, they will be more likely to discuss their interpretations with others online. There is a discussion tool included in most wiki services to aid in this process. This wiki idea might spark good conversations over differing responses to a book. Just think of the possibilities.

4. Classroom guidelines

What if your students were allowed to help formulate your classroom rules? Maybe they do so already. A wiki is the perfect tool for you and your students to collaborate in creating the environment you work in every day.

5. Travel and extra-curricular suggestions

You might create a wiki for students to document their travel experiences. The front page could list locations by state, region, or continent. Links would take visitors to pages created for each location where students could provide travel tips, must-see destinations, restaurant and hotel recommendations, and share their most memorable experiences.

Other extracurricular activities could be documented on this wiki as well. Students will enjoy keeping others updated about their favorite sports teams, suggesting activities for the upcoming weekend, or sharing ideas for science fair projects.

This is another idea that could be opened up to other contributors. Just be sure to screen and monitor all contributions.

6. Bad example wiki

In order to teach students to be critical of what they read on the Internet, you might create a wiki that is wrong on so many levels. Make wild and unsubstantiated claims. Include links to sources that do not go where they are supposed to (otherwise known as "broken links"). Write a paragraph with obvious bias, then have students identify and correct errors and bias in the wiki. This exercise will help them view all Internet sources with a critical eye.

All of the activities suggested so far are for your own classroom wiki. Here is another wiki activity to try with your class. Go to Wikipedia and register for an account. This will give you the privilege of initiating a new Wikipedia article. Once you are a member, think about a special location, personality, or event in your community. When you decide on a subject, search for it in Wikipedia, and if the article does not exist, create one. Then write about some of the history behind what you have chosen. Once the article is posted, invite your students to take part in developing the article. They will catch on very quickly, plus it will give your students an amazing sense of accomplishment to watch their article grow as others around the world get involved.

Now it's your turn to determine how a wiki will best enhance your classroom instruction. The possibilities are endless, so start experimenting with a free wiki service today. Your students will benefit both now and in the future from this experience, and your peers will consider you on the cutting edge of technology.

Podcasts

#50112—*Blogs, Wikis, and Podcasts, Oh My!*

Podcasting is an activity that you and your students can engage in creatively together. Podcasts allow audio and video broadcasts to be saved, sent, subscribed to, and played at any time and anywhere.

PODCASTS: GETTING STARTED

Podcasts are audio or video content that can be downloaded on a computer or fed to a mobile music player (iPod or other MP3 player). Podcasting allows anyone to create and self-publish a syndicated online broadcast or video program. Even conventional radio and television programs can be podcasted, giving them a new way to distribute content.

Podcasts are easy to produce using free software. They are easy to distribute via the Internet, and they are portable so you can listen to them when and where you want. If they are attached to a blog or wiki, your audience can give feedback. It is another way for you as an educator to tap into a technology many young people are already using.

Most podcasts are saved as MP3 files. An MP3 file is just another type of file format used for the compression of music files so they can be played and fit onto such devices as iPods or other MP3 players. You may already be familiar with PDF files, text files, or Excel and Word files. You can now add MP3 files to that list.

Another characteristic of a podcast is that it is an audio file others can subscribe to using RSS. Technically, a podcast is not a podcast unless it is being subscribed to via RSS. If there is no RSS involved, a podcast is simply an audio file. RSS is a way to help you stay updated on your favorite podcasts, blogs, or other frequently updated websites. We will cover RSS feeds in the next chapter. A podcast is usually posted somewhere on the Internet, and others can subscribe to it and download it onto their computer or their portable audio player.

Below are two options for recording podcasts through your computer or even from your cell phone, but first, you will need to download software from one of these providers. Each site offers instructions for installation and operation. You will also need a microphone for your computer in order to record your audio.

- Audacity: **http://audacity.sourceforge.net**

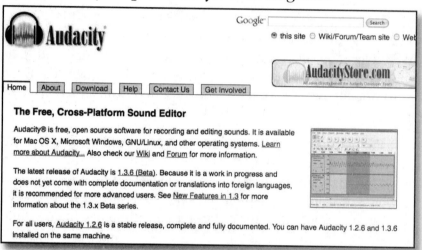

- Garageband: **http://www.apple.com/ilife/garageband** (Macintosh only)

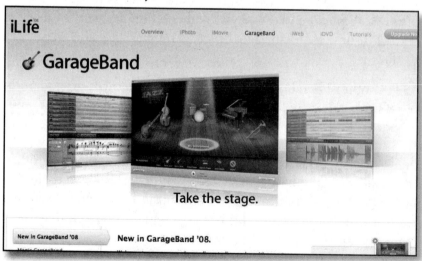

The resource below can be used to create podcasts from existing audio files. Whether you create your own files using Audacity or Garageband, or simply upload files that already exist, GCast is an easy tool for uploading files and creating a podcast.

- Gcast: **http://www.gcast.com**

PODCASTS: IN THE CLASSROOM

Podcasting gives students and teachers a voice—literally! Here are some ideas for creating podcasts using your own audio. Remember, you can also produce podcasts with content created by others. We will discuss a number of possibilities in this section.

1. Newsletter

Inject some life into your weekly report to parents by putting it in the form of an audio or video podcast. Students can take turns starring as the anchor. You might even divide it into segments: a math update from Brian, a science minute from Amber, and this week's birthdays by Manny. Students of all ages can do this—even kindergartners. The audio file, along with a text version, can be sent in an email to parents as well as posting the entry on your blog.

2. Presentations

Podcasting is an excellent way to present student work. In the third part of her project with middle school students, Mary Beth Murgatroyd turned to the Garageband podcasting service. It proved to be the perfect capstone to a process that began with blogged discussions, moved to wikis for organizing and creating a presentation, and finished with a podcast for putting it all together in an attractive and engaging format. Her students worked in groups to create a presentation in the form of a newscast. They learned how to record their voices, add sound effects and music, and then merge it all together.

Murgatroyd found that once she decided to jump into the unfamiliar world of technology, she did not have any trouble receiving support from other teachers and IT staff at her school. What surprised her was the level of engagement and effort her students invested in this project, and the rave reviews received from parents when they saw the final results.

3. Homework

A sixth-grade teacher in Boise, Idaho, has found a way to use podcasts for his students every day (Forester 2008). With a grant from the Qwest Foundation, Richard Whittaker equipped all of the students in his class with iPods. He then downloaded lessons onto their iPods which included the following: video clips, quizzes, music, books, and homework assignments.

Whittaker reported that his students were more engaged, and he credited the tactic with improved performance and higher test scores. He also noted that the use of school-owned iPods leveled the playing field for students who may not have access to a home computer or Internet.

4. Out sick or daydreaming

If you have students who are absent from school, a podcast might be just the remedy to prevent them from getting too far behind in their schoolwork. You could record instructions, lectures, and class discussions to post on your class blog or wiki. If you do this regularly, students might consult these podcasts even if they were in class. Have you ever wished you had a recording of your instructions for a particular assignment? With podcasting, you can say it once, record it, and know that nobody can claim ignorance.

As with blogs and wikis, podcasting opens up a world of possibilities for you and your classroom. The potential is as deep as your own imagination, so dive in and try it for yourself.

CHAPTER 5

RSS Feeds, Skype, and Social Bookmarking

#50112—*Blogs, Wikis, and Podcasts, Oh My!*

In this chapter, we explore three additional technologies that many teachers have found useful either in their own lesson preparation or as a classroom tool.

RSS FEEDS

RSS (Rich Site Summary or Real Simple Syndication) is a simple yet amazing tool that has the ability to streamline the way you view many of the websites you may visit on a daily basis. Getting started with RSS is very easy because there are only two requirements: an aggregator and a feed. Once you have these two, you're off to the races.

An aggregator is a piece of software that takes in all of the ugly XML pages that you have subscribed to and places them in a form that is easy to read, all in one location. Think of an aggregator in the same way you think of an email program that brings all of your email into one place. As with email programs, there are two main types of aggregators from which you can choose. Computer–based aggregators run on a single computer while web–based aggregators are globally available on the Web. There are a variety of aggregators to choose from, and all of them are slightly different. Here are some of the leading RSS tools:

- Bloglines: **http://www.bloglines.com**
- NewsDesk: **http://www.wildgrape.net**
- NewsGator:
  http://www.newsgator.com/individuals/default.aspx
- NewsIsFree.com: **http://www.newsisfree.com**
- SharpReader: **http://www.sharpreader.net/**

Our preference is the first, Bloglines, a web-based aggregator, and the following discussion is tailored to that service. To set up an account in Bloglines (**http://www.bloglines.com**), begin by clicking on the **Register** link on the top right corner of the page.

- Bloglines: **http://www.bloglines.com**

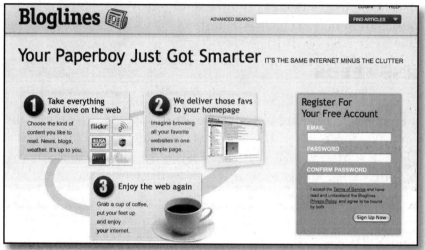

You will be taken to a form that asks your email address, your preferred password, and a few other easy questions. Once complete, click on the **Register** button, and you will receive an email asking you to confirm your account. Upon confirmation, you will be taken to a page that allows you to select some new feeds where you can start receiving content. You can choose to add some of these feeds now, or you can simply go to your aggregator's main page by clicking on **Feeds** on the top left corner of the page.

Usually, these updates contain a headline, a brief description, a URL to the full story being summarized, a date, and the creator's name. By now, you might be thinking that this does not sound all that amazing or interesting, so let's put it another way. Think of the four or five most intelligent teachers you have ever had. Now, add in all of the people you respect and read about daily. Combine those with yet undiscovered people who have similar interests to yours. Finally, mix in a variety of news sources that you rely on to get news that interests you. Take all of this information, funnel it into one location (without constantly having to search for it), and you can begin to understand what

RSS has to offer. Once you grasp the concept of RSS and start to make its use a part of your daily routine, you will feel as if you have never learned so much in your life. You will quickly see that your RSS feeds have the potential to become an extremely valuable source of professional development.

If a site has an RSS feed, it will tell you. Look around the site. Sometimes, an orange badge that says RSS or XML represents RSS. On other sites, you will simply see text that reads, **Subscribe to this site by RSS**. You can find feeds pertaining to most interests that you might have. Additionally, all blogs and most major news sources also publish their content with RSS feeds.

Once you are finished registering for Bloglines and have found the first feed to which you wish to subscribe, click on the **Add** button on the top of the left column of the Bloglines main page. You will see a space in the right column where you can paste in the URL of the website that contains your desired feed. After you type in the URL and hit **Subscribe**, you will possibly see a few different options to select. These options are the various "brands" of RSS (RSS, RSS2, Atom) to which you can subscribe. Using any brand of RSS has proven successful, so simply select one. Then, you can take the time to organize your feeds by creating folders from the drop-down menu.

When you are ready to subscribe, press the **Subscribe** button. If for some reason the feed cannot be read, go back a step, select a different brand of RSS feed, and try again. Once successful, you should see a feed on the left side of your screen that has the name of the source to which you just subscribed, as well as the number of feeds currently waiting for you, in parentheses. You can add or delete as many feeds as you like.

If you are familiar with how to do a search on Google or Yahoo, you are ready to get RSS feeds of your news searches. Simply visit Google News (**http://news.google.com**) or Yahoo News (**http://news.yahoo.com**) and perform a news search.

For example, visit one of the two search sites and search a topic (example: blogging + literacy). Once you click **Search**, you will see all of your results. You can improve your results by refining your search terms just as you normally would in Google or Yahoo.

As with blogs, you can subscribe to podcasts through RSS. Whenever a podcast author posts a new podcast, you can receive it in your aggregator. Sometimes you can even listen to the podcast without ever visiting the site. Try this: subscribe to NASA's podcast, **http://www.nasa.gov/rss/NASAEdge_vodcast.rss**, and marvel at the information you can now access.

It doesn't stop here. Many other sites are RSS-enabled and their resources can be brought into your aggregator. You can collect photo albums from Flickr (**http://www.flickr.com**), bookmarks from Delicious (**http://delicious.com**), and much more. This tool quickly becomes a vital component when teaching a concept or skill, and it allows students to search for sites that are coherent and aligned to their research. As a teacher, you can utilize the RSS feeds to aggregate the blogs that all of your students create.

SKYPE

A newer tool available, Skype (**http://www.skype.com**), proves to be a tool you can easily use on a daily basis. Basically, Skype is a phone service that lets users make computer-to-computer phone calls to anyone in the world absolutely free using your Internet connection. Imagine the possibilities. With this tool, you can collaborate and connect globally with family, other classes, and professional peers using a familiar vehicle—a phone call.

To use Skype's basic service, all you need is a microphone and a set of speakers, but regular users of Skype will encourage you to purchase a headset with a noise-canceling microphone attached. The reason for this is simple. The noise-canceling microphone will get rid of a lot of background noise, and the headset will prevent the person you're connected to from hearing themselves through your speakers while they are conversing with you. Beyond this, you need only the Skype program that can be easily downloaded onto your Windows, Macintosh, or Linux computer.

- Skype: **http://www.skype.com**

Once Skype is installed, launch it for the first time, and you will be prompted to set up your Skype account. You'll need to fill in some basic information and decide on your Skype name. This Skype name is similar to the name type you might use if you were choosing an instant messaging alias, and it is the name other Skype users will employ to contact you. (We do not recommend that you use your full name.)

To search for Skype users, click on the **Magnifying Glass** at the top of the Skype window. At this point, a new window will open, allowing you to search for other Skype users by their Skype name, email address, city, state, or country. When you locate the Skype user for which you are searching, click **Add** to include that user in your Skype buddy list. On the other end, your buddy will get a message asking him or her to approve you and add you to his or her Skype list. If he or she accepts you, you are in.

Skype has a few features that you will want to explore. To make a regular phone call, click on a user in your Skype list and press the **Call** button. On the other end, your buddy's Skype program will ring just like a regular phone. If you and your buddy both have Web cams, you can add video capabilities to your Skype calls. For instant messaging, click on a buddy in your Skype list and press the **Chat** button. Now you can chat through instant messages as you would through any other instant messaging program. To send files, select a user in your buddy list and press the **Send File** button. Skype will prompt you to browse for the file you wish to send. Select the file and send. If your buddy on the other end approves the file, it will be directly sent. Finally, you and up to nine of your contacts can collaborate on a conference call.

All of the uses of Skype mentioned so far are free. There are some additional options that can be used by paying a nominal fee: SkypeIn, SkypeOut, and Skype Voicemail. SkypeIn allows you to register up to 10 local phone numbers based in many cities worldwide. Those friends you register can call you on Skype via their phones. For example, if you have several friends who live in London, purchase a local London number, and they can all call you for free. You must pay a subscription fee to purchase a SkypeIn number, and people trying to call you will pay regular local and/or long distance fees. SkypeOut allows you to call friends on their landlines or cell phones from your Skype program. This service has a flat rate-per-minute fee.

If you are at a loss to find other classes with which to Skype, consider visiting a classroom exchange site like ePALS. On ePALS, you can search for other classes with which you can collaborate. Once you have chosen a class and have established a relationship with them, tell them about Skype and invite them to join.

Here are just some of the ways that Skype can be used with students:

- Have foreign language students participate in Skype conversations with students in other countries.

- Allow students working on a collaborative project to participate in a conference call from various locations.

- Use Skype to exchange documents with project partners.

- Encourage students to present their work to an authentic audience, for example, to other classrooms around the world or professionals in their community.

- Let parents listen in on their children's presentations.

- Set up interviews with an author whose book your class is reading. Send an invitation to the author, inviting him to join Skype and talk to your class.

- Invite a guest speaker to talk to your class via Skype.

So, you have become involved in podcasting, and you have downloaded Skype to make connections with others from around the world. Now, you need to know how to bring these together. Actually, it is quite easy to record conversations and upload them to a class website, blog, or podcast series.

Encourage the other party to install Skype on his or her computer. Then simply make a free call using Skype from your computer to his or her computer. When you are ready to begin your Skype interview, call the other party. Do not limit yourself to only one other person. Skype allows you to start a conference call with up to 10 people (yourself included). To start a conference call, open Skype, click on the **Call** menu, and choose **Start a Conference Call** on a Mac or click the **Conference** button on a PC. Select the individuals to include on your call. At the end of your call, stop the recording process, and save the file as an MP3. Now, you can open and edit your file within Audacity or GarageBand. Don't forget to post your edited file on your blog or class website.

SOCIAL BOOKMARKING

If you use the same computer daily, chances are you have a list of favorites or bookmarks that you have saved and compiled within your browser over time. Your favorites or bookmarks are a quick list of websites that you visit on a regular basis, or they are great resources that you found at one point and might want to revisit. The problem is that if you switch computers throughout the day, your list of bookmarks does not travel with you.

Enter Delicious (**http://delicious.com**). This social bookmarking tool allows you to keep a list of your bookmarks online, which means you can access them from anywhere you have an Internet connection. Be aware that it also permits others to access bookmarks you may want to remain private. So instead of adding bookmarks right onto your computer, you now enter them into a Delicious account. That way, no matter where you are in the world or what computer you are using, you can still access all of your resources. And you can share them with others as well.

- Delicious (**http://www.delicious.com**)

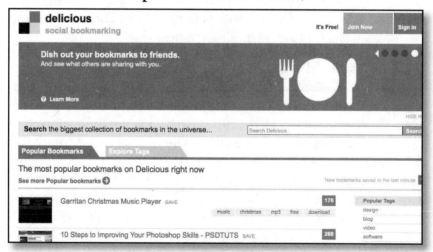

Setting up a Delicious account is easy. Simply click on the **Join Now** button at the top of the page. You will need to create a username and password, and enter your email address. Your email account will be used to validate your registration. Others, when sharing resources, will view your username, so choose one that colleagues and students will remember, but don't give your first or last name.

Next, you will be taken to a page where you have the option to install Delicious browser buttons into your browser toolbar. It is recommended that you install these buttons because they will make accessing your bookmarks and adding new ones a much easier task.

Once the buttons have been installed, you will be prompted to quit and restart your browser. After doing so, you will be taken to an installation confirmation page where you can click on the link and view your saved pages.

Finally, be sure to check your email for a message from Delicious. This message will contain a verification link that you can click for final activation of your account. Clicking this link will navigate you to a Web page confirming successful registration of your account. Now click on the link to the Delicious homepage. Here, your bookmarks will be stored as you save them.

When you find a site you wish to bookmark, click and drag your mouse to highlight some key text on the Web page. This key text might be an important quote or passage, or it might be a description of some sort. Now click the **Tag** button in your browser toolbar. A window from Delicious, containing several boxes, will pop up. You will see that the URL box and the description fields are filled in. Take charge and feel free to change what is in the description box, but don't change what is in the URL area, or your bookmark will not work. Also, you will see that the notes section contains the text you highlighted. You can add more to this box, such as your own ideas and/or other notes about the site you want to remember. You'll also see a field called **Tags**. A tag is a keyword that describes the site you are bookmarking. Enter as many tags as you want, but remember to separate them by spaces. You can select your own tags, and you can choose from suggested tags that will be provided. When you are finished, click the **Save** button, and your new bookmark will be saved into your Delicious account.

After you have saved a few bookmarks, log on to your Delicious account. **Sign In** is in the upper right hand corner. You will be taken to your bookmarks page where you should see the bookmarks you have already saved. This is the main administrative page.

Use the menu bar in the top left corner to navigate around your account. The link to your network lets you add people to your network and allows them to see your bookmarks after they establish a Delicious account. Once added to your network, you can also view their latest bookmarks, which proves to be an efficient method of monitoring the websites your students are bookmarking. By simply adding their Delicious account name in the provided box, they will become part of your network. You can even generate working groups and assign the students specific websites or resources.

Another feature is subscribing to tags, or keywords used to describe bookmarks. When a new bookmark is saved by anyone on Delicious, and that person uses your subscribed tag, you will receive it here. You also have an area with links that people on your network have saved for you. You can use a form on this page to post a link to Delicious instead of posting from the browser button that you installed. However, if you are ever using someone else's computer without this button, the form may be the only way to bookmark a new link.

In the top right corner are some other links to help you manage your account. The **Settings** link allows you to configure Delicious to your liking. You will also find a **Sign Out** link, which will log you out of Delicious. The **Help** link will take you to the online documentation for Delicious, but the online help may be brief and not entirely useful. It will cover all of the functions of Delicious and should answer most of the questions that arise when using the service.

Other links on the page will take you to popular tags and recent bookmarks that route you to a page listing of currently popular and most recent links and tags within Delicious.

Look at the first bookmark that you saved and you will see the name of the link you bookmarked. If you click on this link, you go straight to the site. Also, you will see the notes that you highlighted when you were saving the bookmark. Then, you can view all of the tags that you have associated with this bookmark. You may see that many other people saved this bookmark. If you wish to discover others who have bookmarked this page and what notes they have saved, click on this link.

This is all part of social bookmarking! We can find out what others who have similar interests see as important. Note that once you start poking around in other people's bookmarks, there is a chance of running across sites that you might prefer not to see.

In general, anyone can access your bookmarks by visiting your page, which is **http://delicious.com/** followed by your username. Knowing that your bookmarks are available for the world to view, there may be times when you want to save a bookmark for your private use only. While Delicious makes a strong push toward sharing bookmarks, you can make a particular bookmark private. Privatizing a bookmark is helpful if you want to save a site but not allow others to see it. This feature must be turned on within the settings area.

Sharing bookmarks with the world sounds great, and doing so can enhance the way you and your students conduct research. But it would be irresponsible to send you on your way without telling you about the downside of all of this. As you know, the Internet is full of people who spend their time inappropriately using fabulous tools like this one. It is important to realize that searching within Delicious, just like searching on the Web, can lead to sites whose input is considered inappropriate. Bookmarked sites within Delicious are only as good as those inputting them.

What about using Delicious within a class setting? I'm sure you will discover other ideas on your own, but here is one suggestion to get you started. Set up a class Delicious page. Make one account, and have all students save their bookmarks to that class account. Teach them to tag so everything stays organized. Then, you can take this one step further. Have your students register for an account in Delicious, and have them all give you their account names. You can go into your account, click on your network, and add each student's account as a member of your network.

As the administrator of this account, you can click through the individual students within your network and check out what they are bookmarking. Have all of the students add your account to their networks (along with other students if they wish), and they can discover what you are bookmarking. With your students in your network, you can utilize a really great feature. You can share sites that you feel might be useful to individual students. After adding students to your network, you will see a new addition to your posting window every time you post a new bookmark. By clicking on your student's username, you can give a link to one or several students. They will see the links that you left them in their accounts under **Links For You**.

You can also utilize a shared tag. Let's say that you have a group of three students at Aloha Middle School who are working together on a project about air pollution. Each student has a Delicious account, and each is working to collect sites on air pollution and post these within his or her Delicious account. Have the students agree on a tag they can apply to all of the information collected. Every time these three students find a valid site, they should post it and tag it with a tag such as "cool app." These three students can subscribe to the tag "cool app" from their inboxes on Delicious and share their findings. As a teacher, you might want to subscribe to this account and post to it as well so that you can keep track of their work.

CHAPTER 6

Concluding
Remarks

#50112—*Blogs, Wikis, and Podcasts, Oh My!* © *Shell Education*

Have you noticed? Things are changing: the ways in which we communicate with one another, the ways in which we entertain ourselves, the ways in which we interact with information from around the world, and the ways in which we teach and learn. How are you handling these changes? How will you deal with them?

In your personal life, you have the prerogative to remain as unplugged as you want to be. But as an educator, you have a responsibility for the minds of students whose future success may depend on their ability to navigate the digital world. The fact is, most of your students are already initiated in the use of tools and technologies of our electronic age. If you can tap into those tools and technologies, their chances of having a meaningful and lasting learning experience will increase.

We have explored three major tools that you should consider adding to your toolbox and a few more technologies that may be helpful to you in your preparation and teaching. We have also provided some resources for you to get started and to investigate further.

If you are thinking about a blog, you should consider the blog's author, audience, and purpose. A blog is best for communicating timely information, promoting discussion, and the display of writing and other student work. We discussed several examples of how a blog could be used in your classroom. You might use it to keep in touch with parents or as a classroom news source. You can use it as a catalyst for discussion. Students can use it to write book reports, report on their weekend or vacation, or any other writing projects that you assign.

A wiki is especially useful for collaborative work when you and your students want to build a body of knowledge together. Some of the ideas we explored include using your wiki as a repository for classroom research on a chosen topic, as a workspace for writing projects, and as a place for you and your students to collaborate on establishing classroom rules and guidelines. Other ideas include a library of reviews, a collection of extra-curricular suggestions and reports, and a "bad wiki" that students can critique and correct.

If you want to go multimedia, podcasting is a good place to begin. Any of the ideas that you come up with for a blog or wiki can be applied to and enhanced with a podcast. Whether it is news announcements, presentations of work, another way for students to do their homework, or a foolproof method for keeping everyone caught up and up-to-date, video and audio will help you do what you do more effectively.

You will not be disappointed in the return on your investment. And the investment is not burdensome. We have introduced you to services that are free on the Internet. As a professional educator, you already budget significant time and creative energy towards lessons and strategies that will engage your students and help you meet your goals. We have provided some ideas to help you start integrating your current goals and strategies into a different medium.

You'll realize the payoff immediately. Your students will be challenged and engaged in new and unique approaches to learning. Critical thinking will become fashionable. You will find that students who may have under performed or been bored will take a new interest in what is happening at school. Writers will emerge from places you least expected. Confidence will bloom, not only in your students, but in yourself. However, beware! Your colleagues may begin consulting with you as the resident expert in all things digital. At least you will be able to help them realize how easily these new resources can be integrated into their lesson plans, and show them how to get started.

The possibilities are limited only by your imagination and willingness to submerge yourself in the world of technology. So don't be afraid. Log on and explore the wonders of cyberspace through *Blogs, Wikis, and Podcasts, Oh My!*

Resources

SECTION A

The list below includes science websites that can be used with students of varied ages. They come from my personal website and all have been checked for accuracy and content (at the time of printing).

- A Guided Tour of the Visible Human: http://www.madsci.org/~lynn/VH/

- Amphibian Research and Monitoring (USGS): http://armi.usgs.gov/

- Animal Omnibus: http://www.animalomnibus.com/

- Aurora Page (Michigan Tech): http://www.geo.mtu.edu/weather/aurora/

- Bat Conservation International: http://www.batcon.org/home/default.asp

- Cascades Volcano Observatory (USGS): http://vulcan.wr.usgs.gov/home.html

- Complete Sun and Moon Data (US Naval Observatory): http://aa.usno.navy.mil/data/docs/RS_OneDay.php

- Duke University Lemur Center: http://lemur.duke.edu/

- Earth and Moon Viewer: http://www.fourmilab.ch/earthview/vplanet.html

- Earthquake Center (USGS): http://earthquake.usgs.gov/eqcenter/index.php

- Earthshots (USGS): http://earthshots.usgs.gov/

- Exploratorium 10 Cool Sites: http://apps.exploratorium.edu/10cool/index.php

- Explore Learning: http://www.explorelearning.com/index.cfm

- Frank Potter's Science Gems: http://www.sciencegems.com/

- Hawaii Department of Education (my page): http://jeff.piontek.googlepages.com/

- Honolulu Community College - Dinosaurs: http://honolulu.hawaii.edu/dinos/dinos.1.html

- HubbleSite: http://hubblesite.org/

- Jefferson Lab: http://education.jlab.org/indexpages/teachers.php

- KidSites—Science: http://www.kidsites.com/sites-edu/science.htm

- Marine Geology (USGS): http://walrus.wr.usgs.gov/pubinfo/margeol.html

- Mars Exploration Program (NASA): http://mars.jpl.nasa.gov/

- Nanoworld (University of Queensland): http://www.uq.edu.au/nanoworld/

- National Geographic: http://www.nationalgeographic.com/

- National Geographic Xpeditions: http://www.nationalgeographic.com/xpeditions/

- National Geophysical Data Center: http://www.ngdc.noaa.gov/ngdc.html

- SeaWorld/Busch Gardens: http://www.seaworld.org/animal-info/index.htm

- SETI Institute: http://www.seti.org/Page.aspx?pid=211

- The Best of the Hubble Space Telescope: http://www.seds.org/hst/hst.html

- The Butterfly WebSite: http://butterflywebsite.com/

- The Fish Information Service (FINS): http://fins.actwin.com/

- The Globe Program: http://www.globe.gov/r

- The Nine Planets: http://www.nineplanets.org/

- United States Geological Survey: http://www.usgs.gov/

- University of California Museum of Paleontology: http://www.ucmp.berkeley.edu/exhibits/geologictime.php

- US Fish & Wildlife Service: Endangered Species: http://www.fws.gov/endangered/

- US Fish and Wildlife Service: http://www.fws.gov/

- Vents Program (NOAA): http://www.pmel.noaa.gov/vents/

- Volcano World: http://volcano.oregonstate.edu/

- Volcanoes (Michigan Tech): http://www.geo.mtu.edu/volcanoes/

- Weather Maps (University of Michigan): http://cirrus.sprl.umich.edu/wxnet/maps.html

- Weather Underground: http://www.wunderground.com/

- Welcome to the Planets (NASA): http://pds.jpl.nasa.gov/planets/

- WhaleNet (Wheelock College): http://whale.wheelock.edu/Students.html

SECTION B—BLOGGING

FREE BLOG-HOSTING SERVICES
- Blogger: https://www.blogger.com/start

- Edublogs: http://edublogs.org/

- Live Journal: http://www.livejournal.com/
- WordPress.com: http://wordpress.com/

HELPFUL BLOGS FOR TEACHERS

- Classroom 2.0: http://www.classroom20.com/
- Support Blogging: http://supportblogging.com/
- Teachers First: http://www.teachersfirst.com/content/blog/blogbasics.cfm
- Weblogg-ed: http://www.weblogg-ed.com

SECTION C—WIKIS

- PBwiki: http://www.pbwiki.com
- Wetpaint: http://www.wetpaint.com
- Wikipedia: http://www.wikipedia.org
- Wikispaces: http://www.wikispaces.com

SECTION D—PODCASTING

- Audacity: http://audacity.sourceforge.net
- Garageband: http://www.apple.com/ilife/garageband (Macintosh only)
- Gcast: http://www.gcast.com
- iTunes: http://www.apple.com/itunes/download
- NASA: http://www.nasa.gov/rss/NASAEdge_vodcast.rss

SECTION E—RSS, SKYPE, SOCIAL BOOKMARKING

- Bloglines: http://www.bloglines.com
- Delicious: http://delicious.com/
- Flickr: http://www.flickr.com

- Google News: http://news.google.com

- NewsDesk: http://www.wildgrape.net

- NewsGator:
  http://www.newsgator.com/individuals/default.aspx

- NewsIsFree.com: http://www.newsisfree.com

- SharpReader: http://www.sharpreader.net/

- Skype: http://www.skype.com

- Technorati: http://www.technorati.com

- Yahoo News: http://news.yahoo.com

SECTION F—SECURITY AND FACT-CHECKING

SECURITY

- Educause: http://www.educause.edu/

- International Society for Technology in Education:
  http://www.iste.org/AM/Template.cfm

- National Cyber Security Alliance:
  http://staysafeonline.org/

FACT-CHECKING

- easyWhois: http://www.easywhois.com

- FactCheck.org: http://www.factcheck.org/

- Internet Archive: http://www.archive.org

- Snopes.com: http://snopes.com/

SECTION G—SAMPLE LESSONS

- NCTE: http://www.readwritethink.org/lessons/index.asp

- Nortel Learn iT.org: http://nortellearnit.org/lessons/
  (free lesson plan downloads)

#50112—Blogs, Wikis, and Podcasts, Oh My! © *Shell Education*

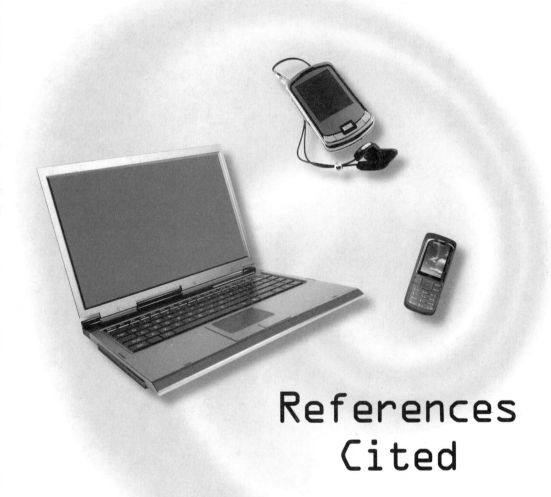

References
Cited

#50112—*Blogs, Wikis, and Podcasts, Oh My!* © *Shell Education*

REFERENCES CITED

Collier, L. 2008. Widening the audience: Students reading and writing online. *The Council Chronicle* (November): 10–13.

Forester, S. 2008. Boise teacher uses iPods in lessons. *The Olympian*. November 22. http://www.theolympian.com/northwest/v-print/story/670661.html.

Morgan, B., and R. D. Smith. 2008. A wiki for classroom writing. *The Reading Teacher* 62 (1): 80–82.

Murgatroyd, M. B. 2008. The many ways of knowing and showing. *Middle Ground* 12 (2): 24–25.

National Council of Teachers of English (NCTE). 2008. Reading and writing differently. *The Council Chronicle* (November): 15–21.

Phillips, S. 2008. Can MySpace make better writers? *Miami Herald*, November 9. http://www.miamiherald.com/news/education/story/756156.html.

ADDITIONAL REFERENCES

Asen, S. 1992. *Teaching and learning with technology.* Alexandria, VA: Association of Supervision and Curriculum Development.

Brown, A. L. 1994. The advancement of learning. *Educational Researcher* 23 (8): 4–12.

D'amico, C. 1997. Workforce 2000 revisited: Work and workers in the 21st century. Indianapolis, IN: Hudson Institute.

Edwards, C. M. 1995. The Internet high school: A modest proposal. *National Association of Secondary School Principals (NASSP) Bulletin* 79 (573): 67–71.

Edwards, O. 2008. Forward thinking: Three exemplary schools reveal the shape of things to come. *Edutopia* 4 (2): 28–31.

Fullan, M. G. 1998. Leadership in the 21st century, breaking the bonds of dependency. *Educational Leadership* 55 (7): 6–10.

Fuller, H. 2000. First teach their teachers: Technology support and computer use in academic subjects. *Journal of Research and Computing in Education* 32 (4): 511–17.

Gardner, H. 1983. *Frames of mind.* New York: Basic Books.

Gardner, H. 1993. *Multiple intelligences: The theory in practice.* New York: Basic Books.

National Institute for Literacy. 2004. Equipped for the future: 21st century skills for the new economy. http://eff.cls.utk.edu/PDF/eff brochure.pdf.

November, A. 2003. *Empowering children with technology.* Arlington Hgts, IL: Skylight Publishing.

Pierson, M. E. 2001. Technology integration practice as a function of pedagogical expertise. *Journal of Research on Computing in Education* 33 (4): 413–30.

Rowley, J. B., and P. M. Hart. 1996. How video case studies can promote effective dialogue. *Educational Leadership* 53 (6): 28–29.

Williams, D. L., R. Boone, and K. V. Kingsley. 2004. Teacher beliefs about educational software: A Delphi study. *Journal of Research on Technology and Education* 36 (3): 213–29.

NOTES:

NOTES:

NOTES: